CW01202594

050000006546 D9

FAMOUS PEOPLE
FAMOUS LIVES

Biographies of famous people to
support the curriculum.

Saint Bernadette

by Nicola Baxter
Illustrations by Peter Kent

W
FRANKLIN WATTS
NEW YORK • LONDON • SYDNEY

SHROPSHIRE LIBRARIES

0 5 4 0 3 6 9 9

First published in 1999 by
Franklin Watts
96 Leonard Street
London
EC2A 4XD

Franklin Watts Australia
14 Mars Road
Lane Cove
NSW 2066

© 1999 text Nicola Baxter
© 1999 illustrations Peter Kent

The right of the author to be identified
as the author of this work has been asserted.

The right of the illustrator to be identified
as the illustrator of this work has been asserted.

ISBN: 0 7496 3347 6

Dewey Decimal Classification Number:: 270.092

A CIP catalogue record for this book
is available from the British Library.

Series editor: Sarah Ridley

Printed in Great Britain

Saint Bernadette

François Soubirous was worried. It was the middle of winter, and his young wife Louise was about to give birth to their first child.

François was a poor miller in a place called Lourdes, in southern France. He couldn't afford to call the doctor.

Luckily, everything went well. Louise gave birth to a tiny baby girl.

"We'll call her Marie Bernarde," said François.

But that didn't last long.

Bernadette, as she was soon known, was not a very healthy child. She was always small and pale, and she suffered badly from asthma. The damp, dark basement where the family lived was bad for her health, too.

In those days, only rich people could afford to send their children to school. Bernadette's parents worried about their little daughter.

What will her future be?

When Bernadette was ten, something happened that made them worry even more. A dangerous disease, called cholera, swept through the country. Many people died.

Bernadette caught it and was soon very ill. Everyone was afraid she would die. Her parents were too poor to afford the doctor's help.

But they did not feel they were alone in their trouble. They were sure that God was looking after them. Night and day, they prayed by the little girl's bed. They prayed to God the Father, to Jesus His Son, and to the Virgin Mary, Jesus's mother.

Very, very slowly, Bernadette got better. Her parents were relieved and happy.

And so, to everyone's amazement, Bernadette grew into a young woman. She dreamed of giving her life to God by becoming a nun when she was old enough.

One winter's day when she was fourteen years old, Bernadette went out to collect some firewood.

As she gathered twigs and broken branches beside the River Gave, Bernadette had no idea that her life was about to change for ever.

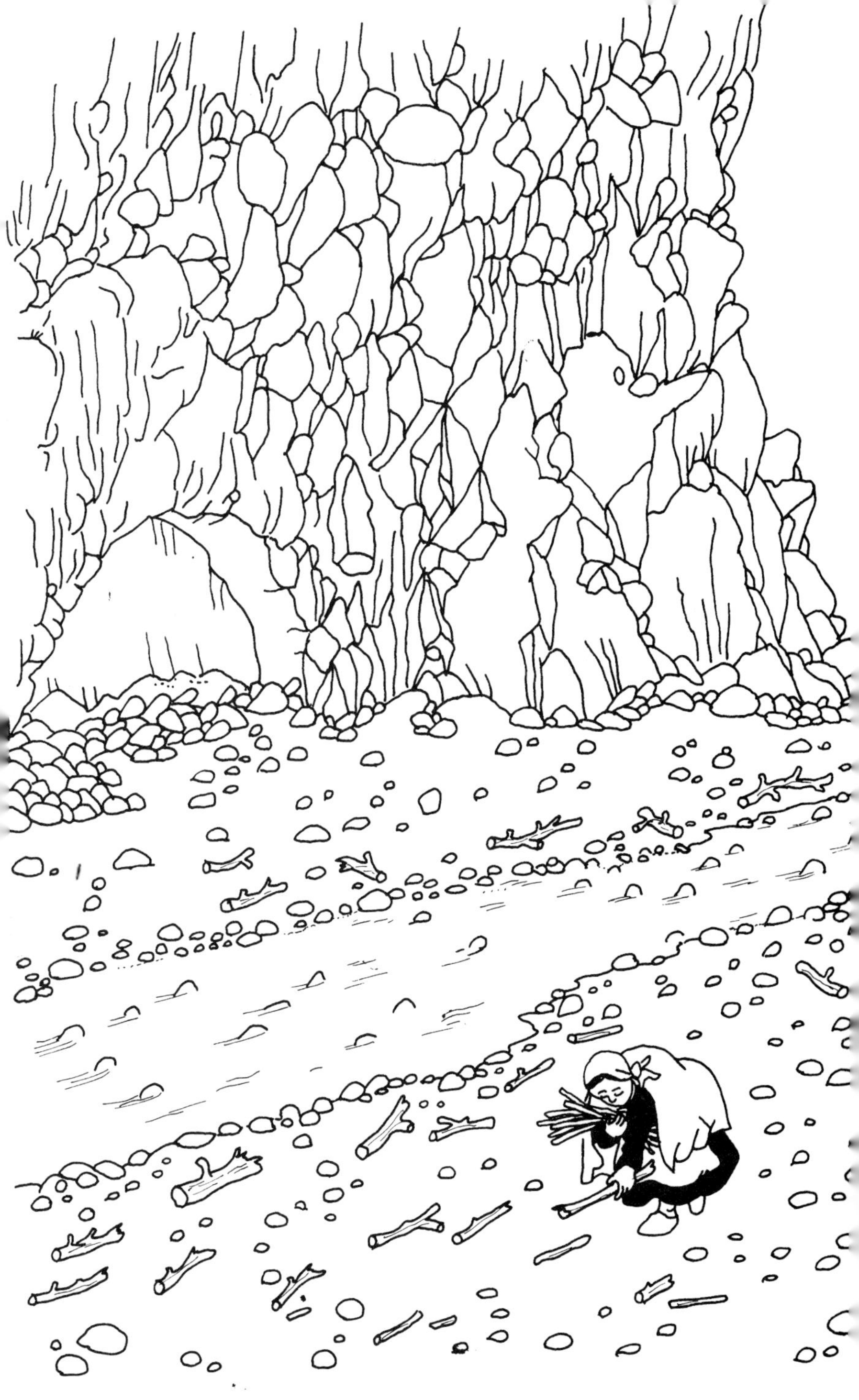

Suddenly, Bernadette realised that she was not alone. She looked up and saw a lady standing at the entrance to a cave. It was almost like a dream, but clever people later called it a vision.

Bernadette fell to her knees in wonder. She could hardly believe her eyes, but she knew that she was not imagining things.

I must remember everything.

The Virgin Mary spoke to her. Although Bernadette could not understand everything she heard, she knew it was important.

I am the Immaculate Conception.

When the vision vanished, Bernadette did not hesitate. She ran to her village, calling to everyone she met.

Something wonderful has happened!

What's the matter with her?

16

Everyone was amazed to see the small, pale girl looking so excited. She told them about the vision she had seen, calling the Virgin Mary 'the Lady'.

But it took a long time to persuade anyone to come with her to the cave.

When at last her friends and relations followed her to the riverbank, most of them were disappointed.

But a few began to believe Bernadette's story. They listened carefully to what she told them.

Over the next few months, Bernadette went back to the cave many times. The Lady often appeared, but only Bernadette was ever able to see her.

At first only a few people followed Bernadette to the riverbank and the cave...

This is probably silly, but you never know...

I've missed my breakfast!

… but each day more and more people came, until there were crowds jostling along the little path every morning.

> She calls herself the Immaculate Conception. I don't really know what it means.

Bernadette couldn't understand why she had been chosen to hear the Lady's words. She knew the Lady's message was important though, and she wanted everyone to hear it.

One day the Lady pointed to a nearby rock. Bernadette saw that clear water was bubbling out of a crack in it.

When the watching people saw Bernadette drinking from the spring, they all wanted to do so as well.

The Lady told Bernadette many things. She spoke about how important it was to pray and to follow God's teaching.

One day she said, "I want you to build a chapel right here."

Bernadette was puzzled. How could she build a chapel? She was a young girl who was not very strong. She didn't even know how to begin.

But somehow she knew that God would find a way to help her.

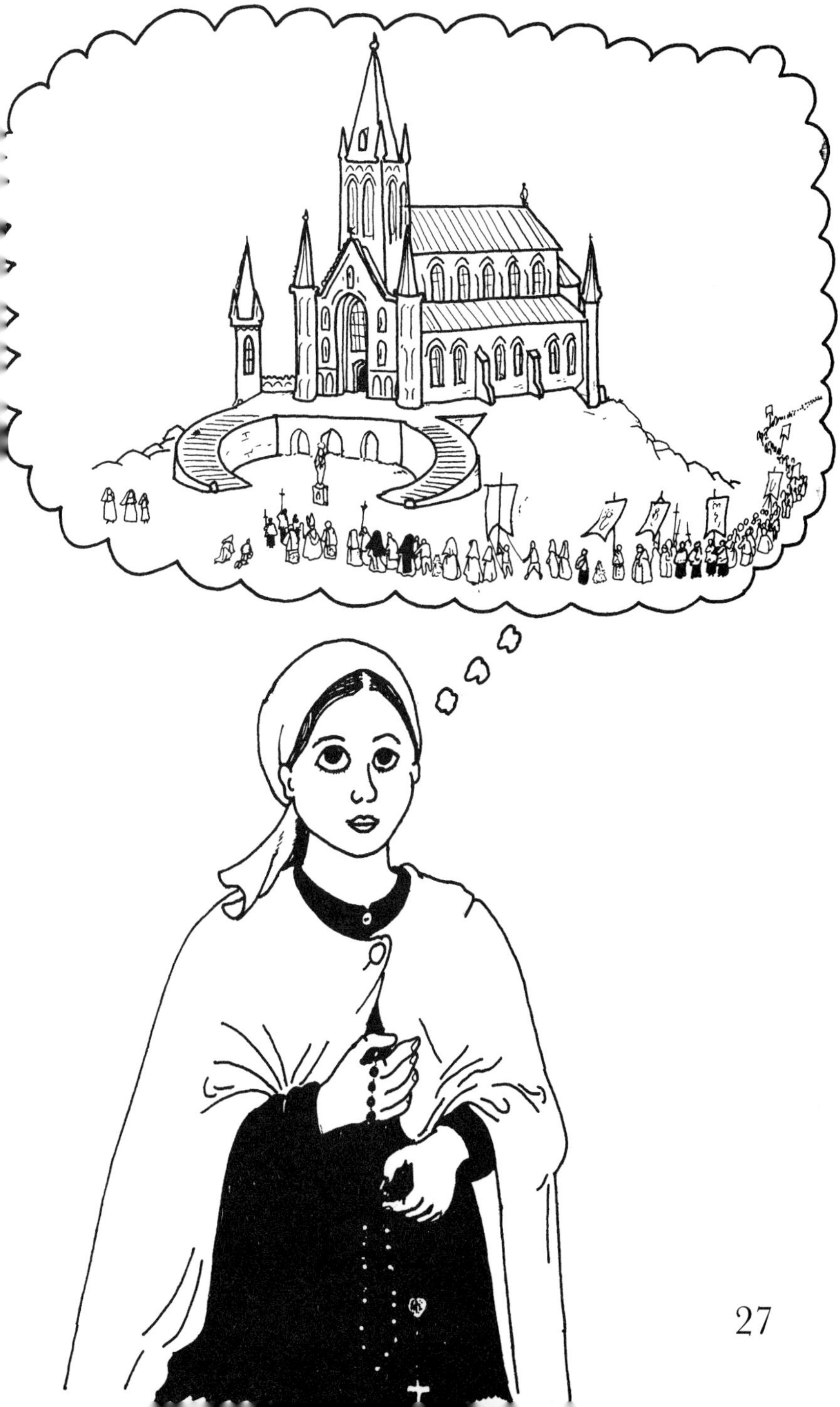

The Lady appeared to Bernadette eighteen times in all. Then, as suddenly as they had started, the visions stopped.

Of course, the crowds only knew this because Bernadette told them. She still went to the cave as often as she could to pray and drink from the spring.

Is it our fault she's not here?

Maybe she will appear again one day.

We can still drink from the holy spring.

News of what was happening at Lourdes soon spread across the country. More and more people flocked to the place where the Virgin Mary had appeared.

Many of the visitors were sick or injured. They hoped that they would be cured if they prayed and drank from the spring. And some of them were!

Meanwhile, important people in the Church heard about the miracles that were said to be happening at Lourdes.

They decided the matter must be looked into urgently.

When Bernadette heard that she must answer questions from such important people, she was worried. She didn't know what to say to clever people who knew so much.

But Bernadette need not have worried. She prayed for help and soon found that all she had to do was to tell the truth.

The cardinals and bishops were impressed by how much she loved God. She never changed her story, no matter how many questions they asked.

She called herself the Immaculate Conception. What does that mean?

She must be telling the truth.

How could a girl who didn't go to school know such a word?

It was not an easy time for Bernadette. The questions tired her out. There was always someone who wanted to talk to her. Her asthma got worse, and she had to spend days in bed.

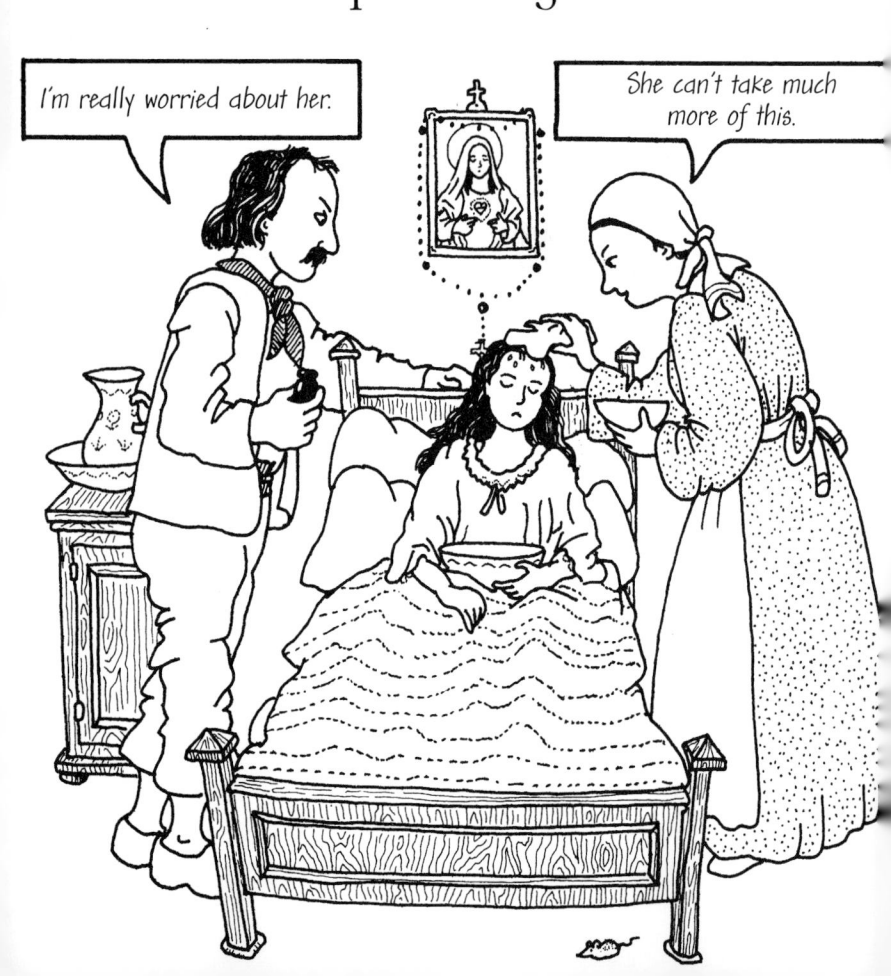

More than ever, Bernadette wished she could become a nun. She would be in a peaceful place, and she could spend her days in prayer.

But the nuns at the convent kindly shook their heads.

"The life of a nun is not easy," they said. "Bernadette is not strong enough to live with us. And she is still so young."

At last the leaders of the Church agreed that Bernadette had been telling the truth. Almost at once, work began to build a large chapel. There would need to be places for the many visitors to stay as well.

And a few years later there was good news for Bernadette too. She had never given up her dream of becoming a nun. When she was twenty-two, she went into the convent at last.

Bernadette was very happy there. She was far away from Lourdes. She wasn't even there when the great Basilica, as the chapel was called, was finished.

Bernadette was only thirty-five when she died. But her years as a nun were full of peace and happiness.

You'd never know she was famous.
AVE MARIA + AVE MARIA
IHS
She's so quiet and good.
It's a shame her health isn't better.

Meanwhile, Lourdes had changed completely from the place Bernadette knew.

Every year, more and more visitors came. They were called pilgrims. As their numbers grew, so did the town.

Even today, thousands of people from all over the world make the journey to Lourdes. They go to services at the Basilica. Often there are so many people that some have to listen outside.

Some visitors take water from the spring home with them. Others dip themselves right into the water!

Does it feel cold, dear?

Many people believe that their visit has made them feel better in their bodies, minds and spirits.

As for Bernadette, she has never been forgotten. In 1933, she was made a saint for her belief in God and the example she gave to others. Many people pray at her tomb in the convent at Nevers.

Further facts

Cholera

When Bernadette was a girl, doctors were only beginning to understand how diseases are spread. Cholera is a dangerous disease that is spread by dirty drinking water and by having open sewers in the streets. It is still a problem today in some countries without clean water supplies and drains.

Pilgrimages

For hundreds of years, people have made special journeys to holy places. Sometimes they have a problem or illness that they want to pray about.

Making a journey shows how important the matter is to them, and takes them away from their everyday life. This means that pilgrims can concentrate on their prayers and feel even closer to God.

Some important dates in Bernadette's lifetime

January 7th, 1844 Bernadette is born in Lourdes, France.

February 11th, 1858 Bernadette has a vision of the Virgin Mary on the bank of a river near her home. Over the next six months she has another seventeen visions.

1866 Bernadette becomes a nun in a convent in Nevers, France.

1876 The large church, or Basilica, at Lourdes is opened.

1879 Bernadette dies in her convent, aged only thirty-five.

1925 Bernadette is beatified by the Roman Catholic Church. This means that she is believed to be in heaven, and people on earth can pray for her help.

1933 Bernadette is made a saint by Pope Pius XI.